Les DeMerle

JAZZ/ROCK FUSION

volume one

REVISED

T0058945

DRUM CENTER PUBLICATIONS

ABOUT THE AUTHOR

Les DeMerle was born in Brooklyn, N.Y., November 4, 1946. He launched onto the New York jazz scene with his own all-star jazz group and performed with Lionel Hampton before age 17. He's recorded five award winning L.P.'s with his poll winning "Transfusion" group, and is featured on the Grammy award winning Harry James L.P. "The King James Version". As a clinician he has appeared in most major music stores in the USA and in Europe. His European clinic tour for Pearl Drums and Zildjian Cymbals set attendance records in England, Scotland, Germany and France. Les also owned and operated his own LA Jazz club, the "Cellar Theatre" which featured some of the world's leading musicians, along with Les DeMerle's percussion ensemble. Les has lived in N.Y. and L.A. and since 1985 has made Chicago his home. He is currently leading the Les DeMerle Band which features the lovely and talented vocalist Bonnie Eisele (Les's wife). He also is busy on the concert circuit with the "Transfusion" band. His latest creative efforts include his new video, "Rock Fusion Drum Set Applications, Volumes 1 and 2", produced by M&K Productions, and his new drum book, "How to Beat the System." *Downbeat* Magazine has stated Les DeMerle drums with fire, speed, imagination and taste. He is definitely a leader in the world of percussion. Les DeMerle is one of the founding fathers of fusion. He is a giant in this industry.

Herb Wong
K.J.A.Z.
San Francisco

THE MUSIC

JAZZ ROCK FUSION is a work which is tightly in
tune with the constant expanding musical levels of
drumming in todays music. It exposes the player
to the coordination and endurance involved in playing a high energy music, and simultaniously prepares
you for the melodic and dynamic aspects of the drum
set now. Writing this music was a great challenge
and experience, and this contribution to music is a
sincere offering of knowledge that I would like to
pass on to you, the player.

IMPORTANT NOTE: Be sure to fully understand the
meaning of all words and musical symbols. Practice
each exercise slowly. Then play the exercises, grooving
on them, repeating them 20 times each. Practice at
a steady schedule.

                              LES DE MERLE

Publisher's Note:

We revised this Edition of Jazz-Rock Fusion Volume I so more practice material could be added. We compressed all of the original Volume I and Les wrote twenty more pages of practice material to prepare the student for the now available Jazz-Rock Fusion Volume II.

DRUM CENTER PUBLICATIONS

This book is dedicated to Darla in appreciation of her constant inspiration and dedication.

Special thanks to:

Tony Galino for copying Volume I

Julie Olfield for copying added material

Dom Famularo and Jerry Ricci for the idea of revising Volume I

Billy Cobham and Bob Livingston

Drum Center Publications for their support.

THE WORK WITHIN

QUARTER-RIDE ROCK STUDIES - CO-ORDINATION EXERISES

RIDE CYM.
SN. DR.
BASS DR.

HI-HAT

TRIPLET FEELS - COORDINATION EXERCISES

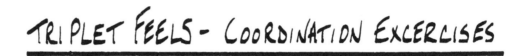

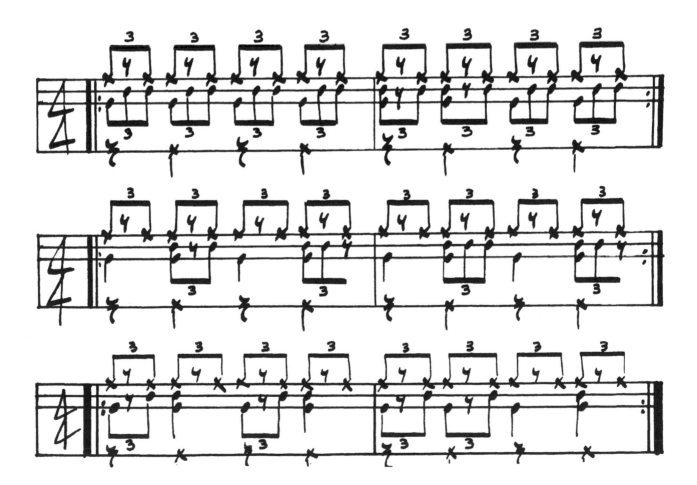

3

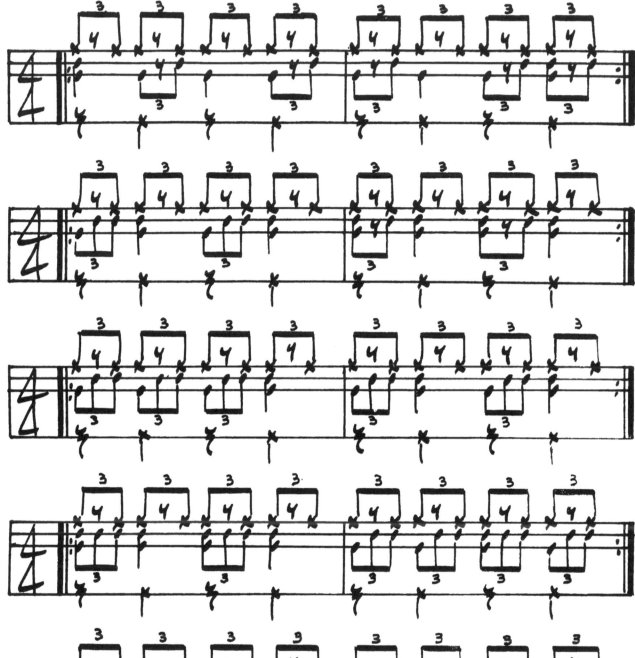

Syncopation- Between Snare and Bass

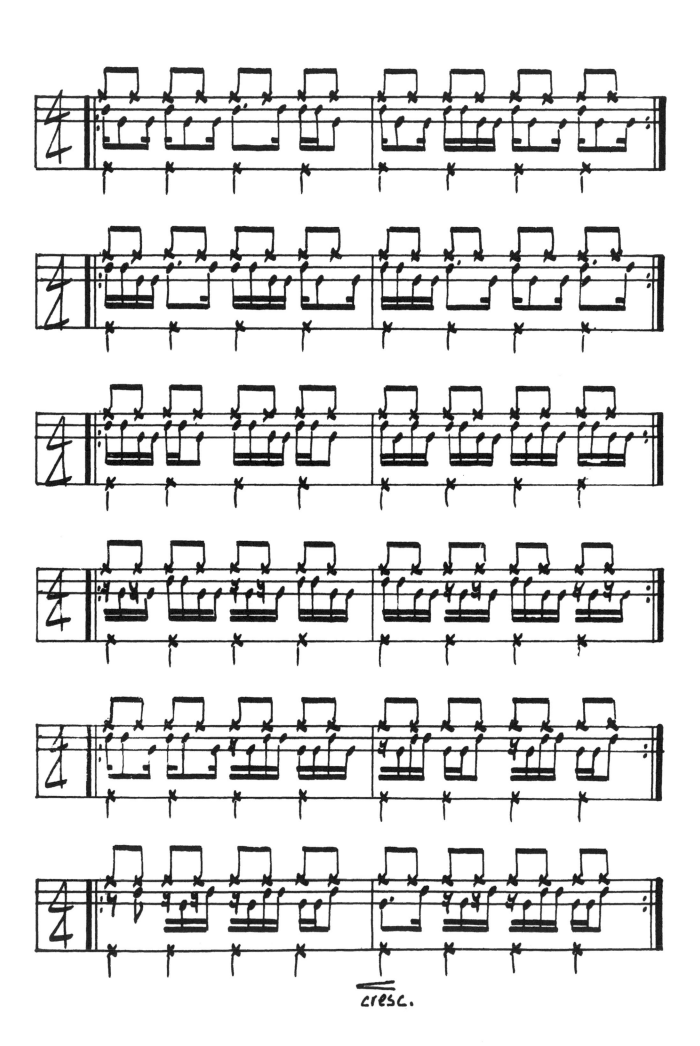

cresc.

5

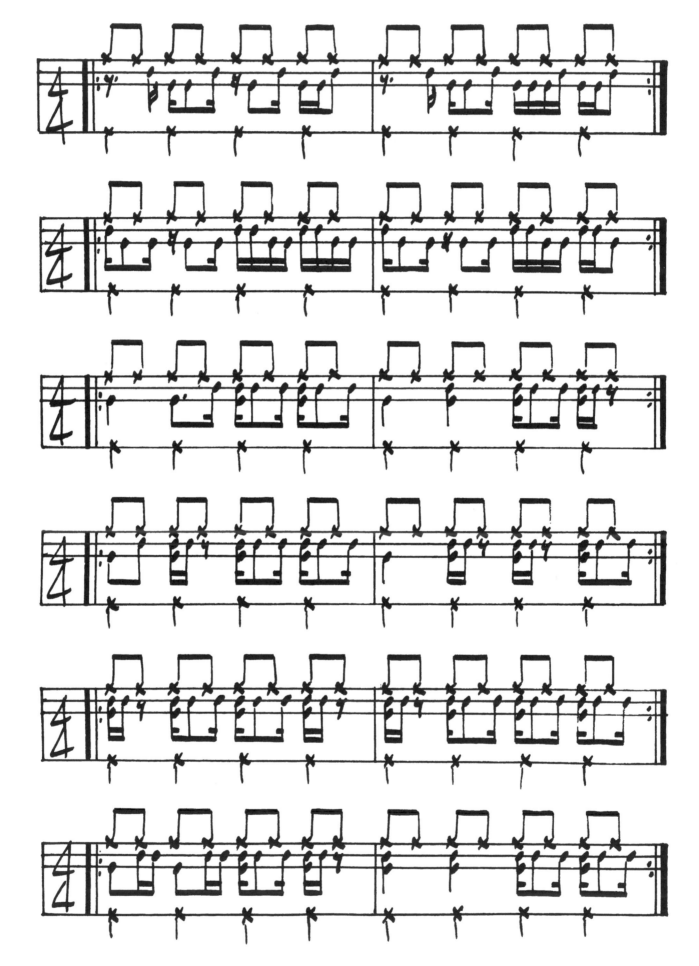

DOUBLE-TIME FEELS (32nd notes)

7

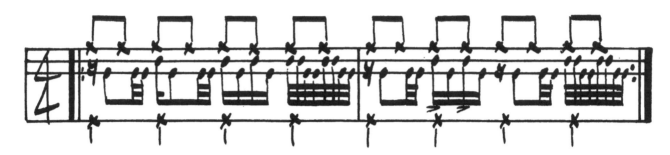

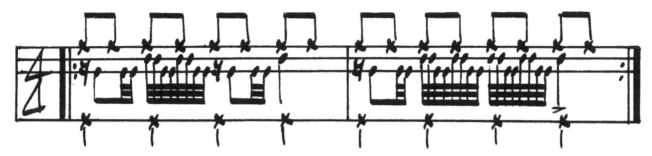

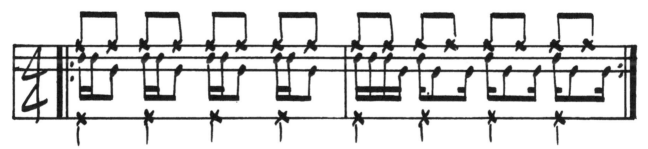

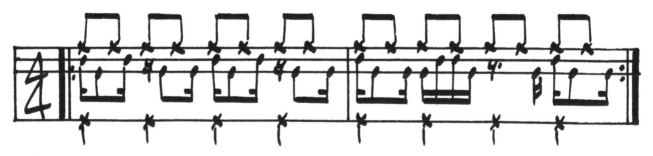

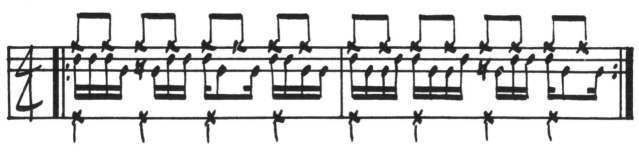

HARD ROCK AGAINST QUARTERS

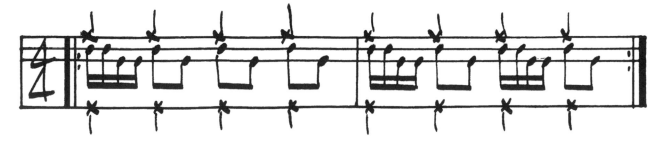

9

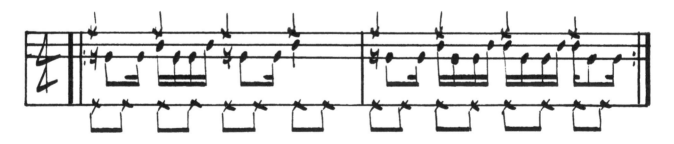

NEW HI-HAT ROCK EXCERCISES W/ SYNCOPATED SNARE AND BASS

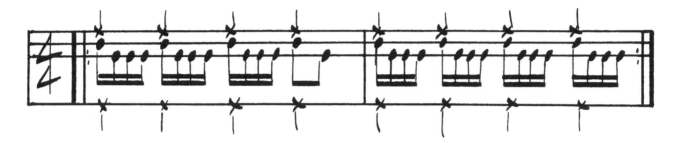

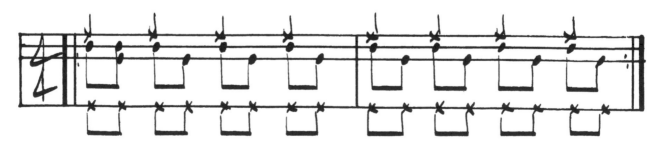

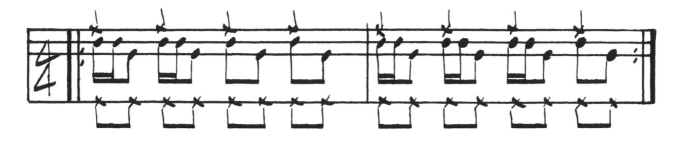

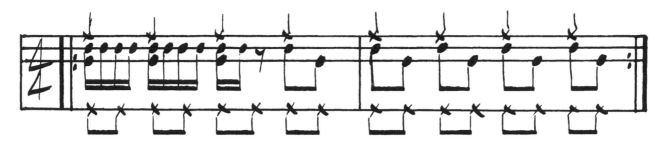

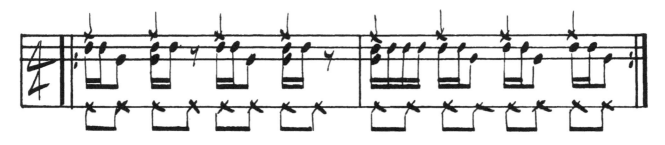

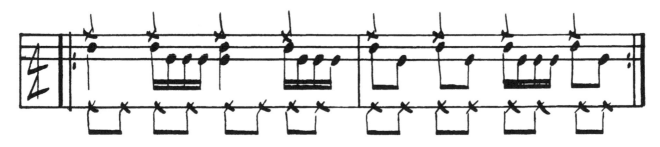

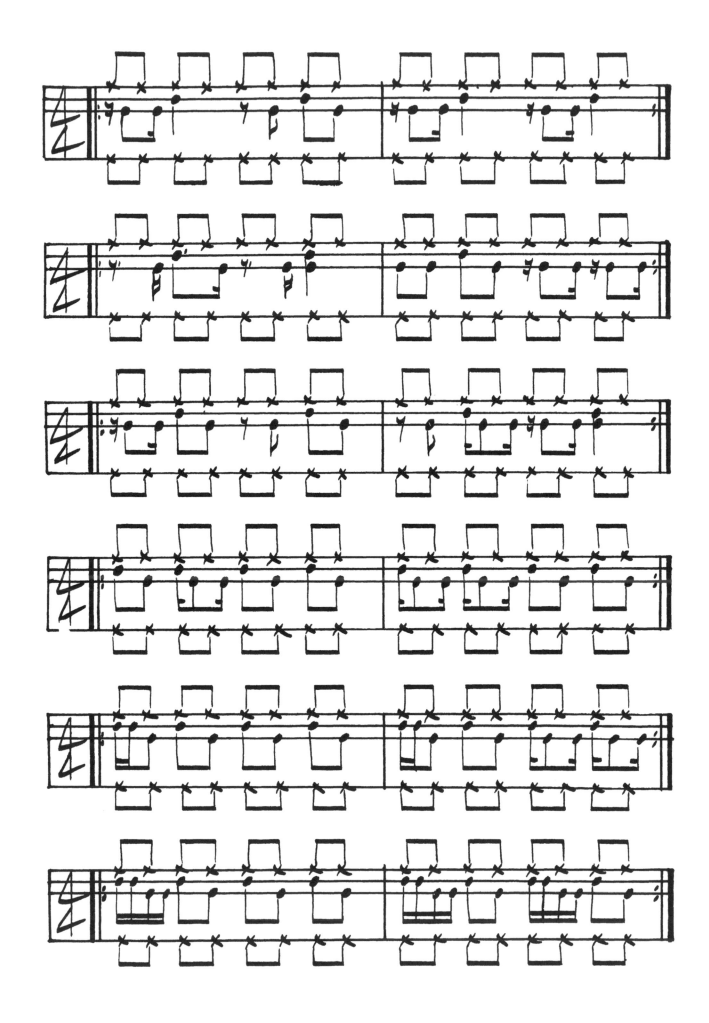

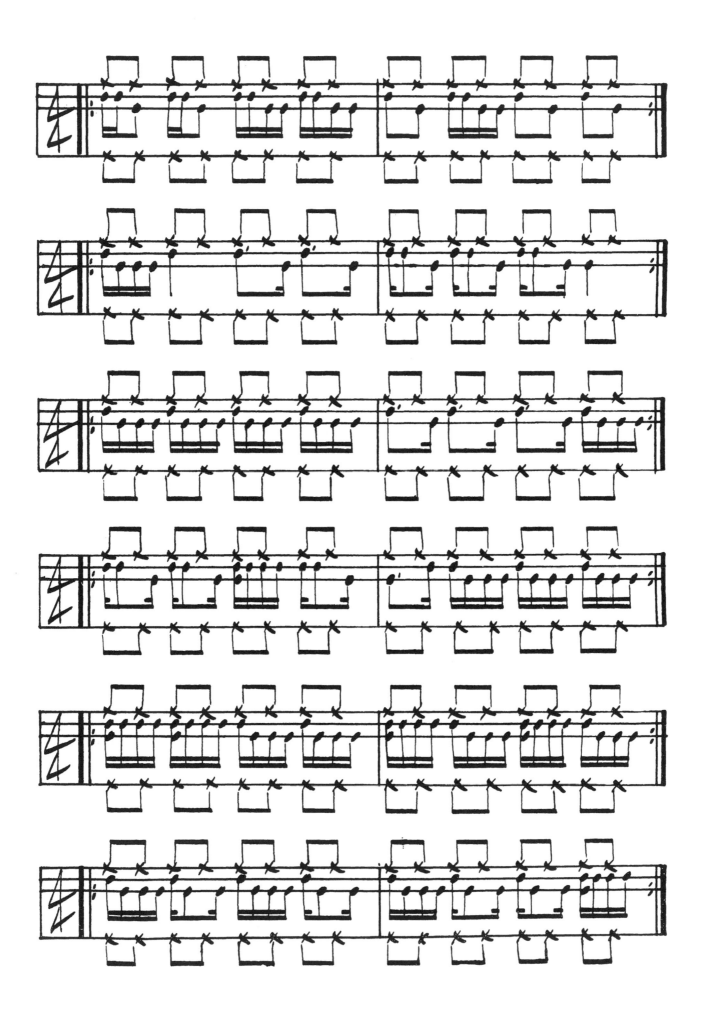

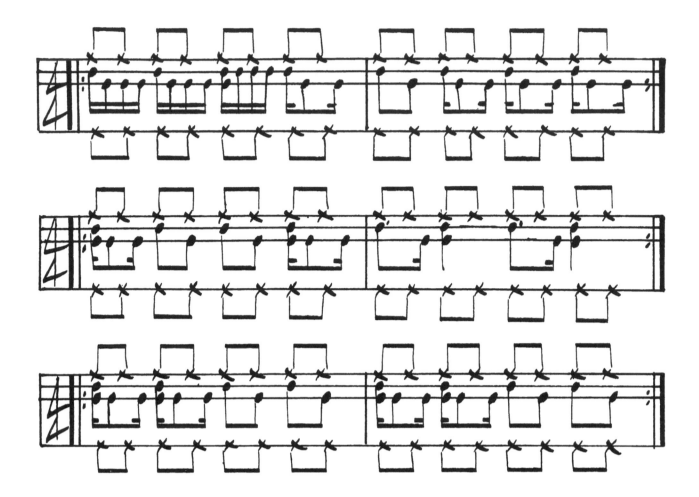

16ᵗʰ-NOTE RIDE EXERCISES in 4 FUSING 8ᵗʰ's in HI-HAT

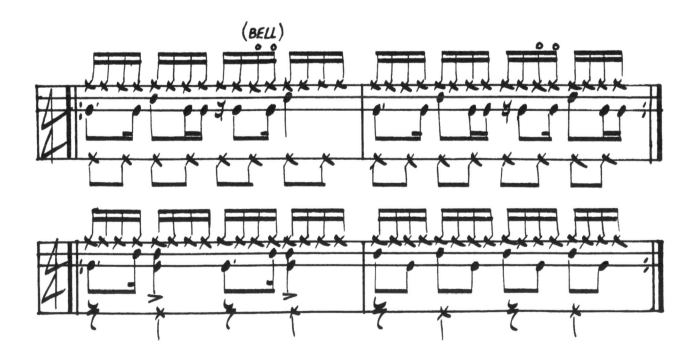

(BELL)

15

16th NOTE ROCK FEELS

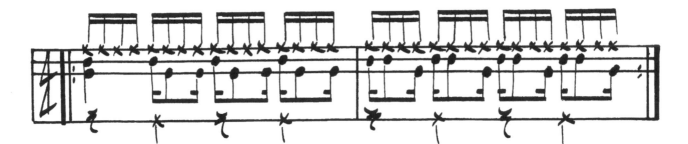

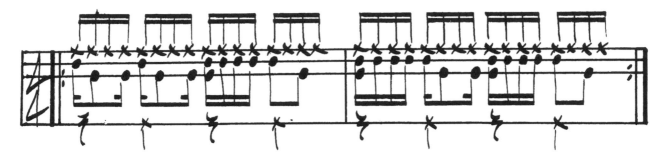

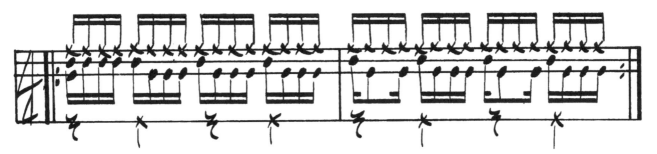

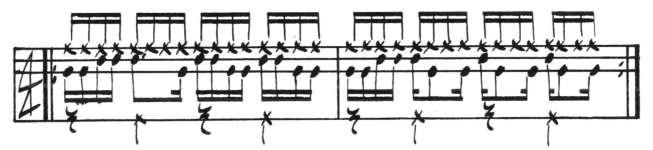

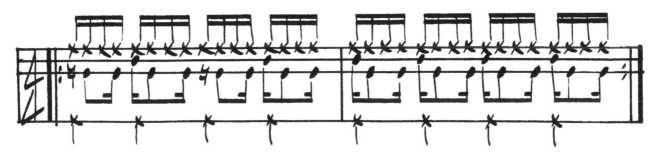

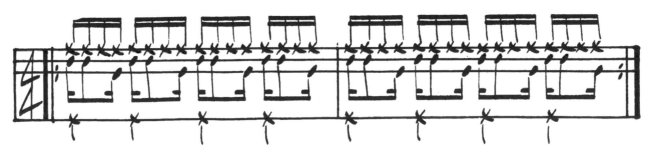

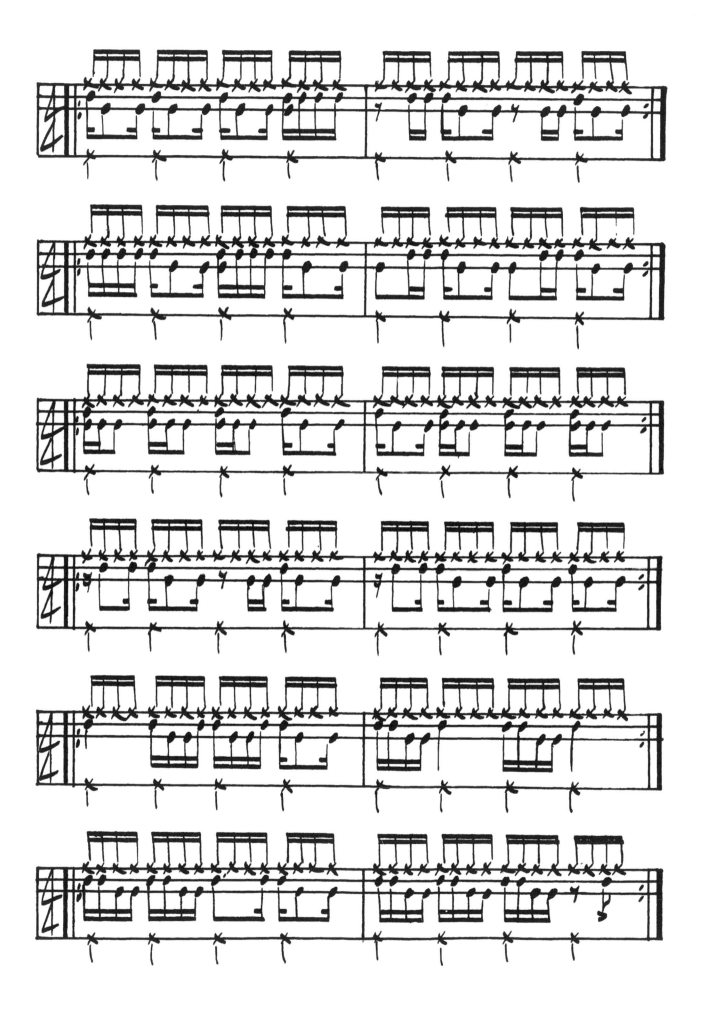

ROCK SYNCOPATED TIE EXERCISES

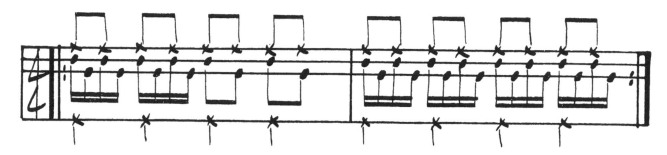

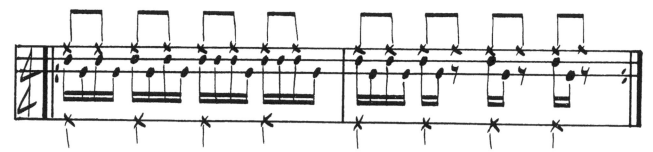

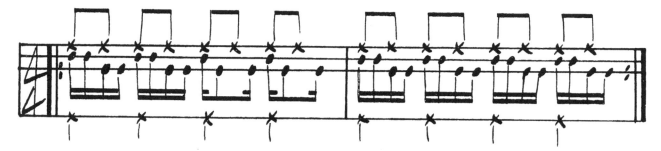

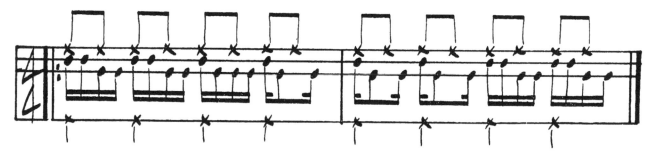

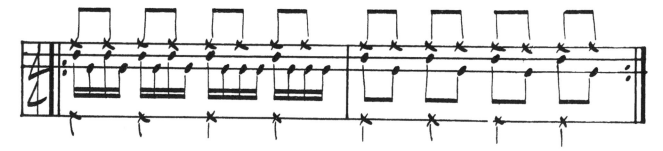

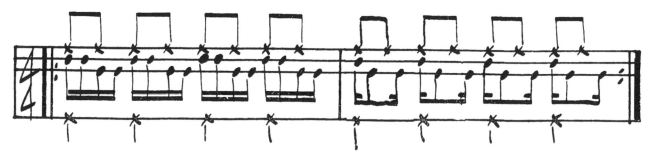

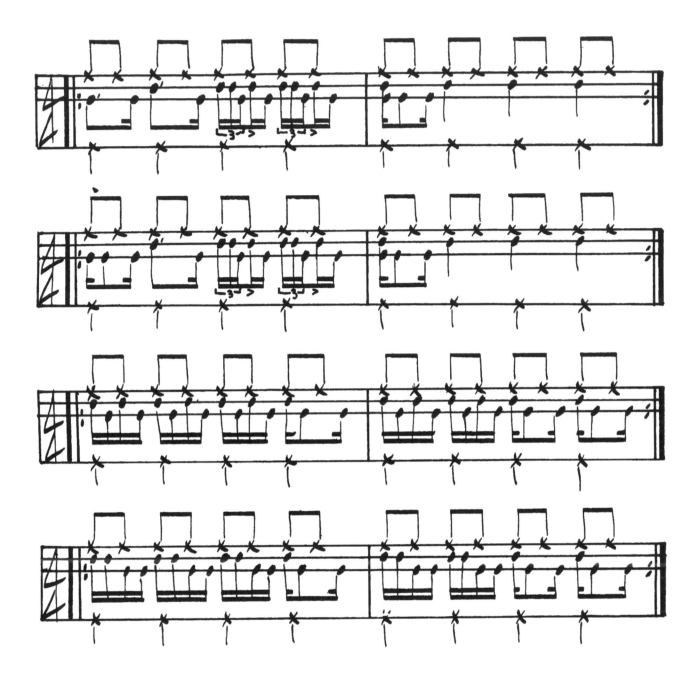

34 Rock Exercises

21

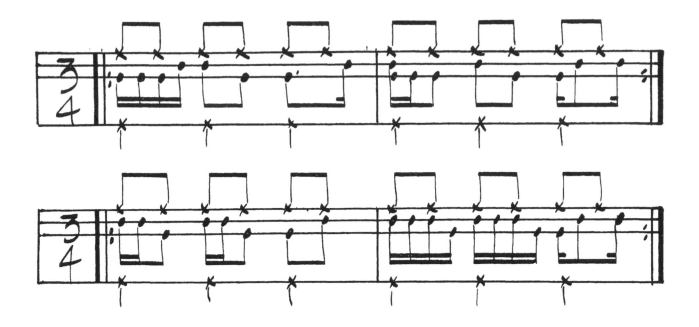

2-Bar Rock Phrasing Excercise - 1 Bar 8ths, 1 Bar 16ths

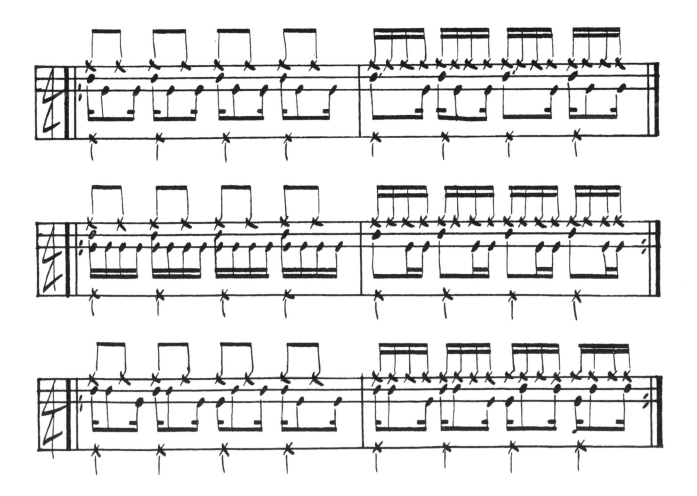

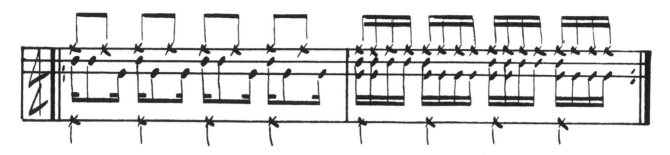

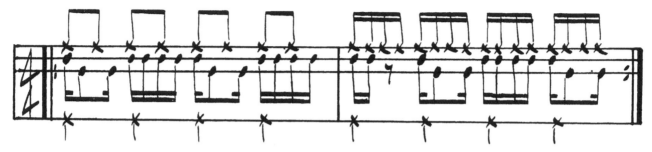

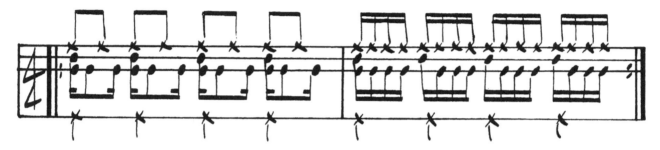

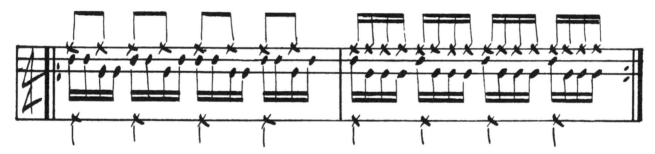

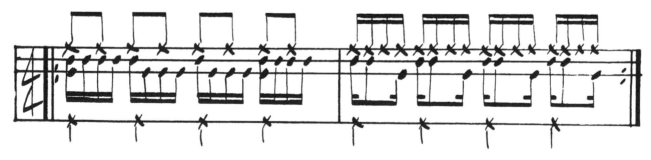

TOTAL JAZZ-ROCK SYNCOPATED RHYTHMS

23

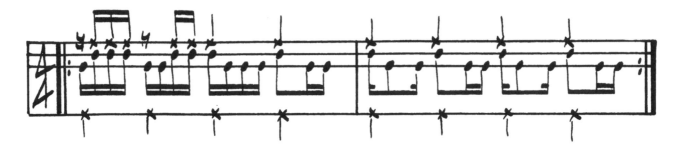

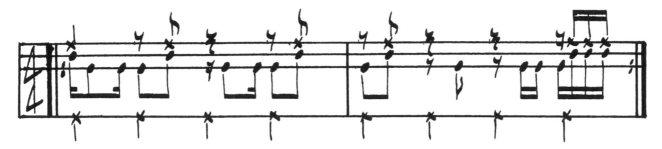

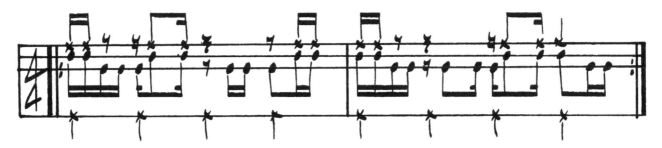

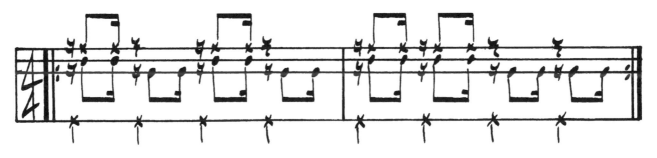

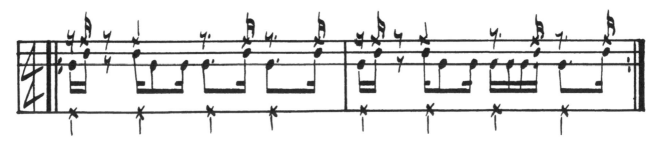

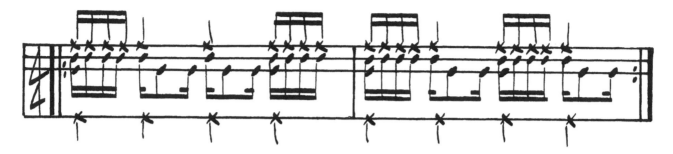

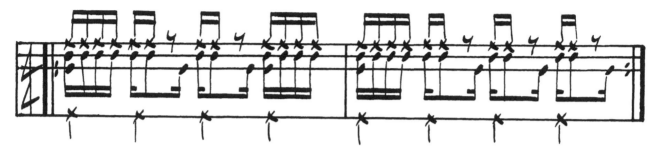

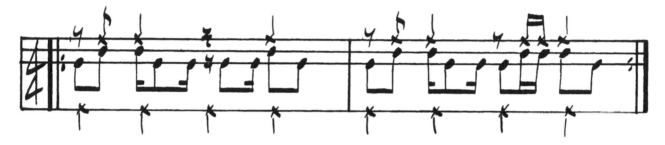

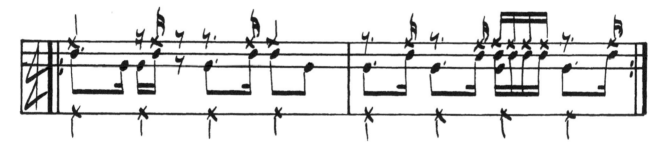

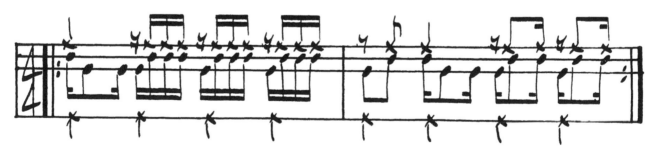

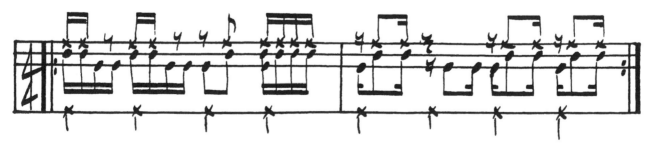

25

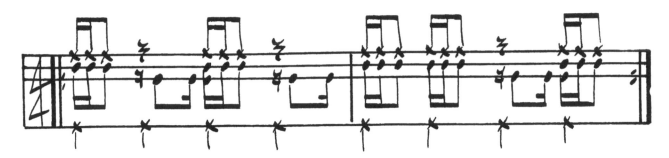

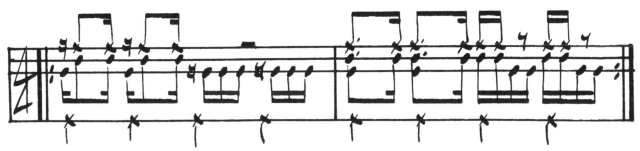

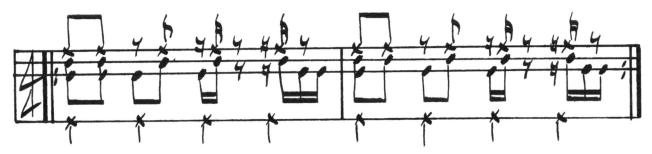

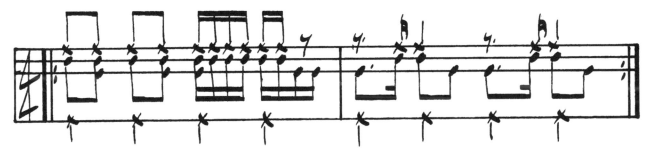

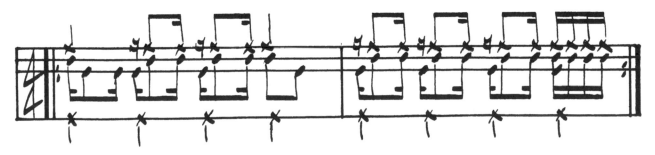

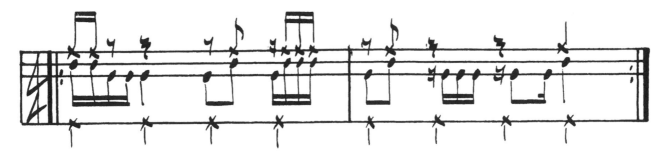

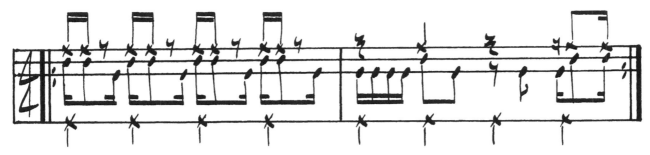

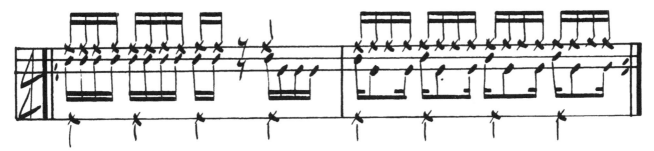

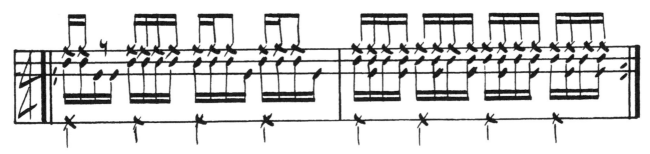

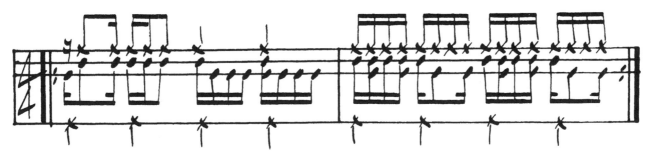

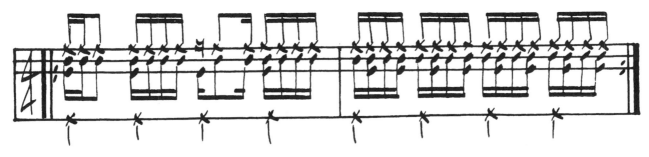

HEAVY ⁵⁄₄-TIME EXERCISES AGAINST ♫ & ♫♫

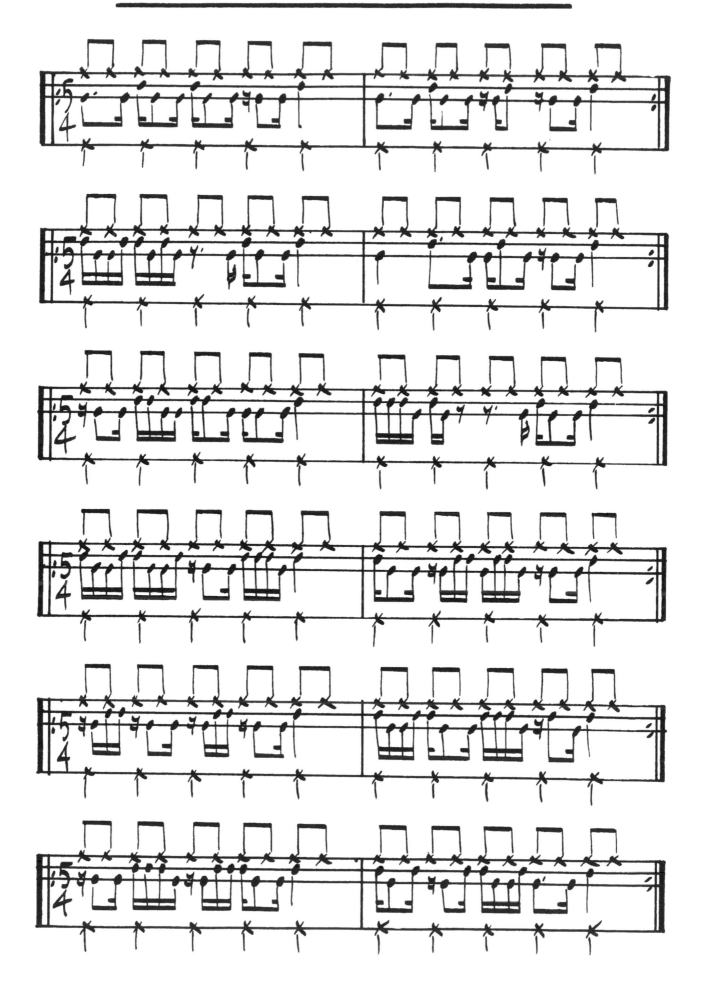

28

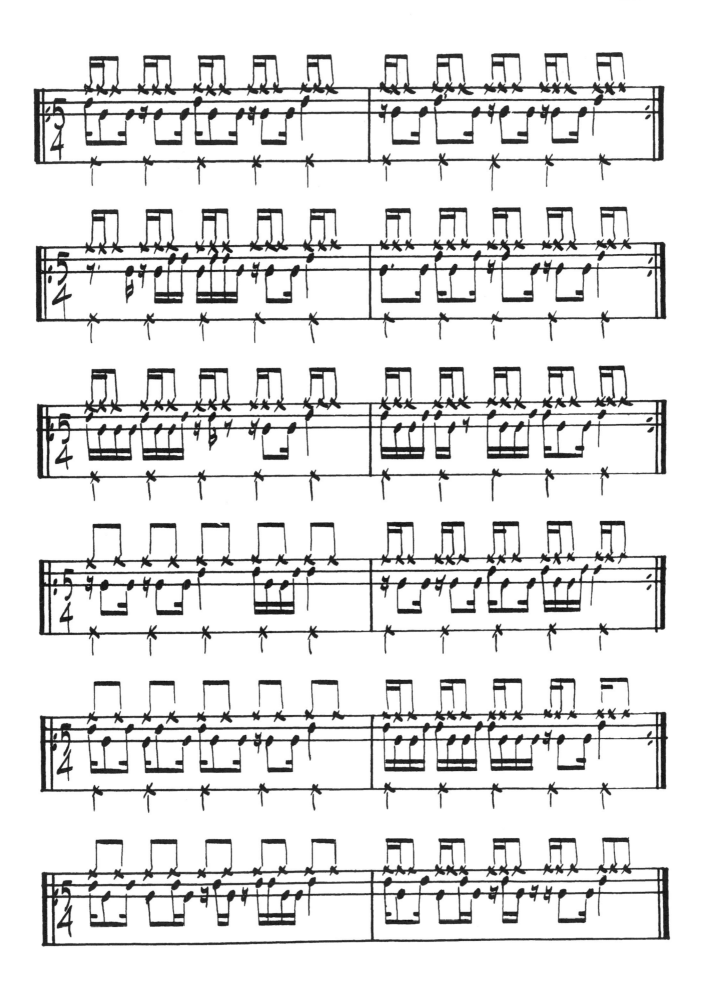

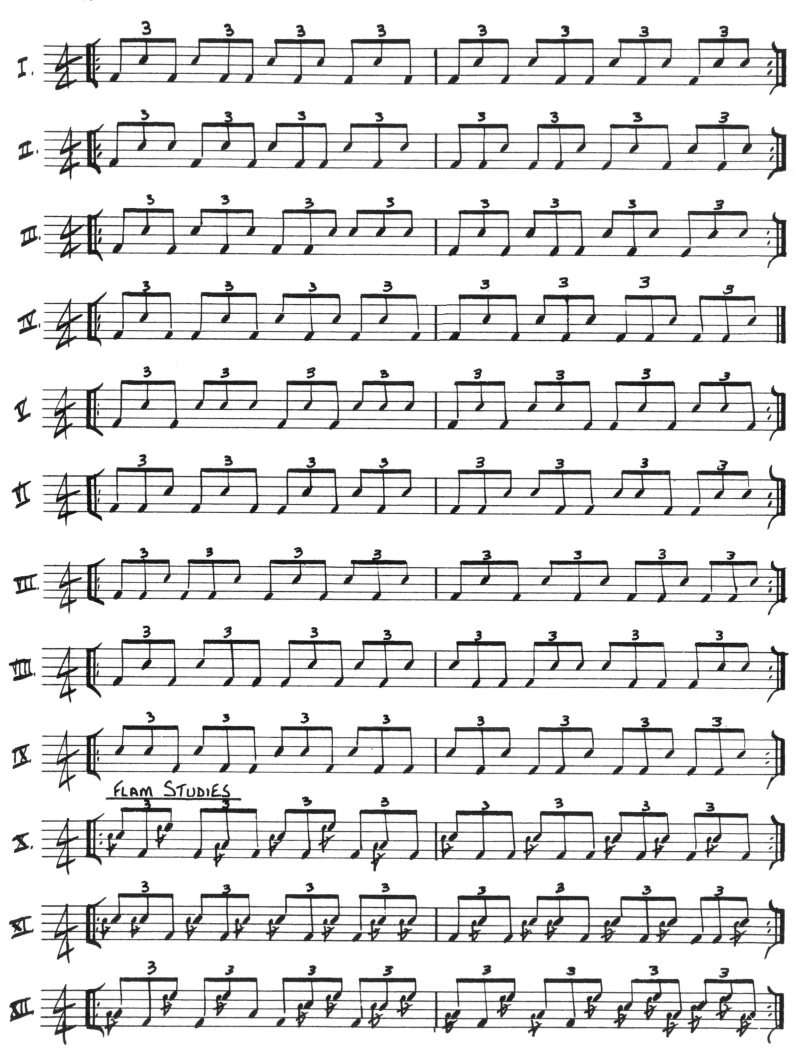

MELODIC SCALES

MELODIC JAZZ

Jazz Rock - Subdivisions - 7/4

NOTE: ON ALL EXERCISES ON THIS PAGE, IMPROVISE SECOND BAR, PLAYING HI-HAT AS WRITTEN IN FIRST BAR.

RIDE
SN
BASS

HI-HAT

NOTE: ON ALL EXERCISES ON THIS PAGE, PLAY EIGTHS IN RIDE AS ALTERNATE

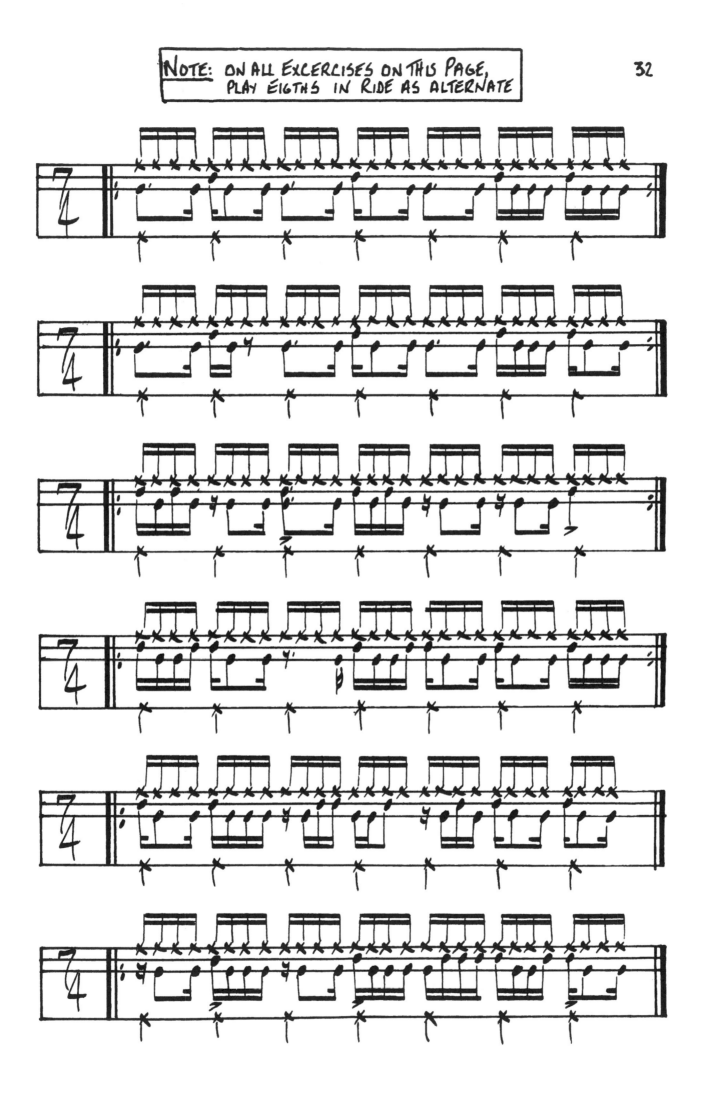

33

JAZZ ROCK - SUBDIVISIONS - $\frac{6}{8}$

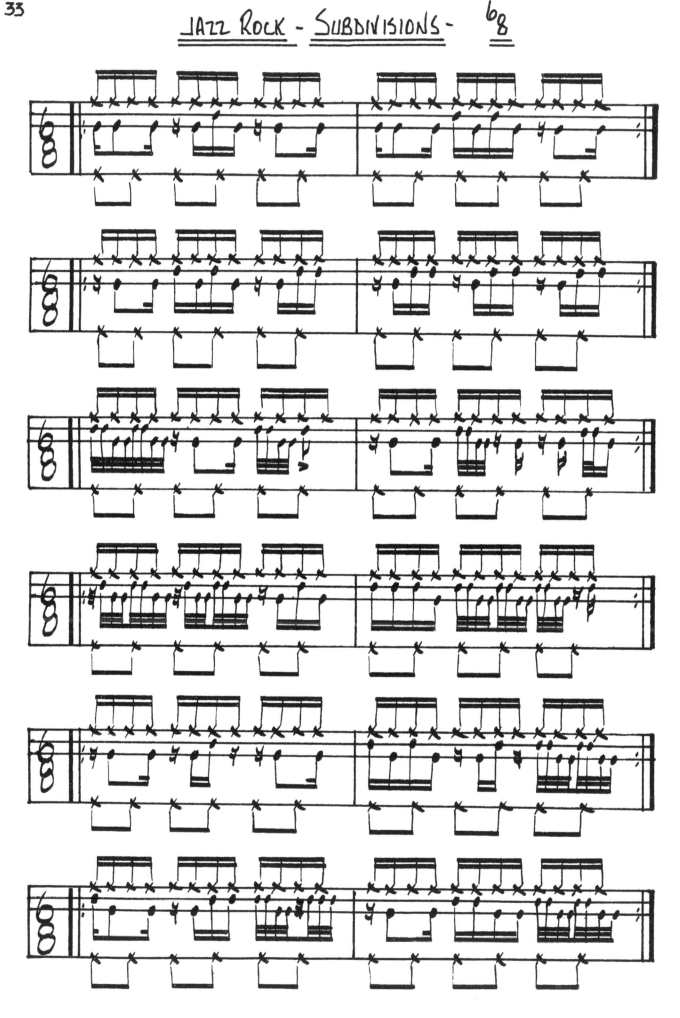

$$\frac{8}{8} + \frac{7}{8} \quad \text{OR} \quad \frac{15}{8}$$

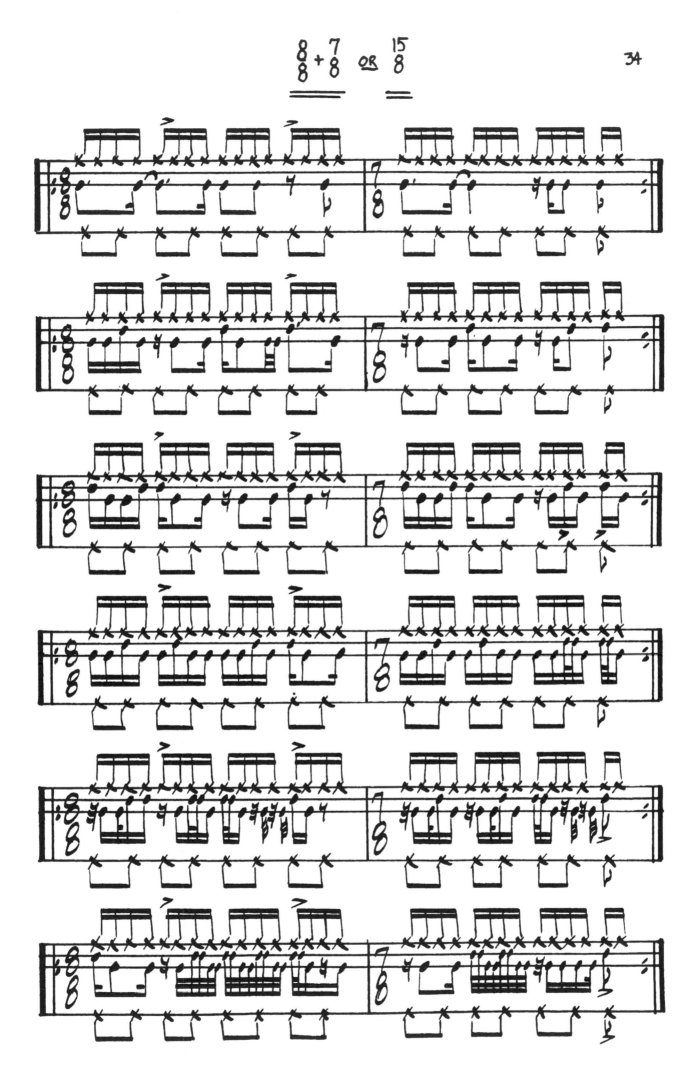

JAZZ ROCK - SUBDIVISIONS - $\frac{10}{8}$

NOTE: PLAY 16ths IN RIDE AS ALTERNATE

PATTERNS & LINES FOR DRUMSET IN 4/4

RIDE CYM.

SN. DR.
BASS DR.
H. H.

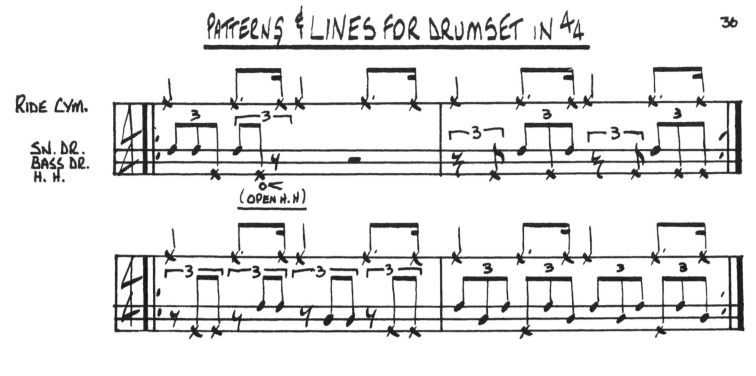

(OPEN H.H)

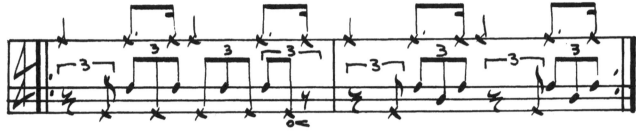

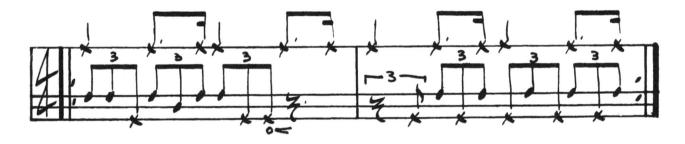

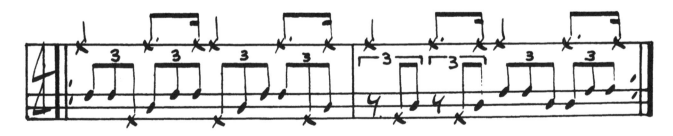

FOUR-BAR LEFT HAND ENDURANCE BUILDERS

FOUR BARS OF TIME IN BETWEEN EACH EXERCISE

MED. TO FAST

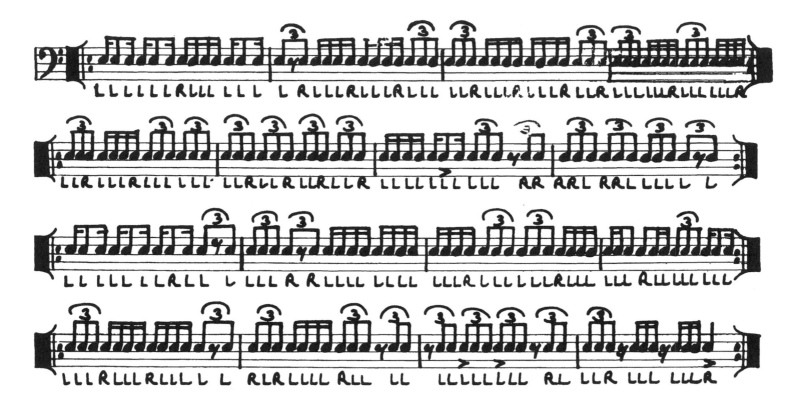

CYMBAL INDEPENDENCE

TWO BARS RIDE — TWO BARS FILL

MED. TO FAST

TWELVE-BAR FLAM SOLO IN A FUNK GROOVE

MED. FAST

41

6/8 Fusion Work

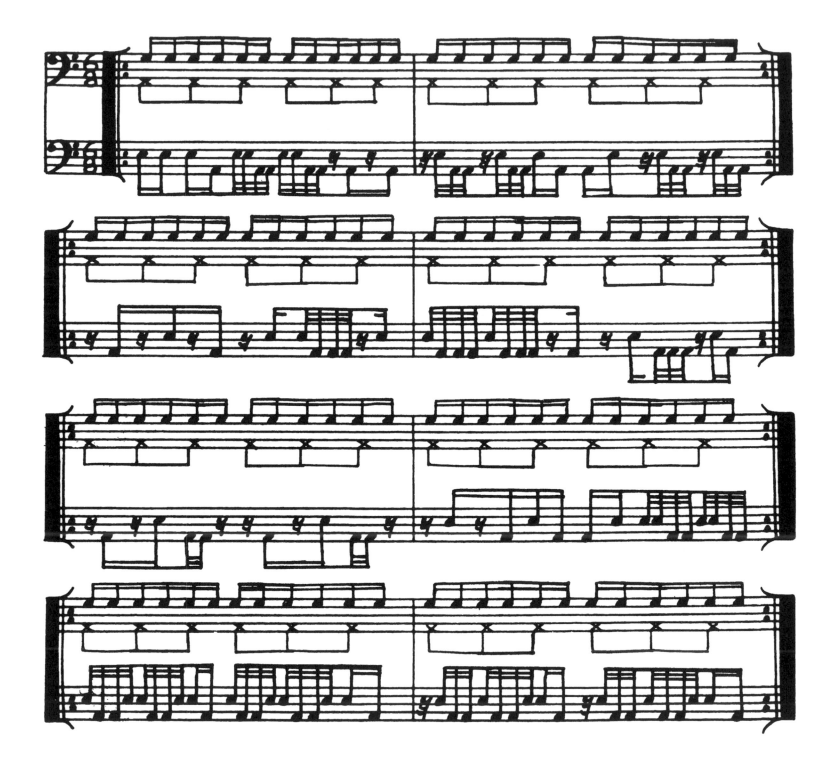

54 INDEPENDENCE WORK

MEDIUM

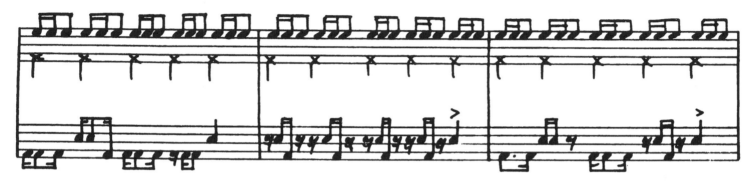

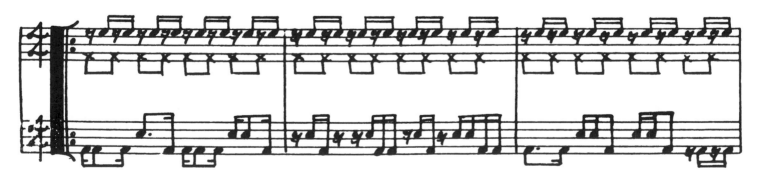

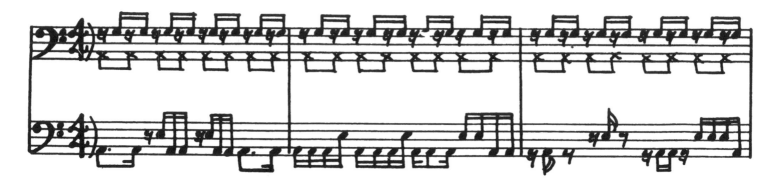

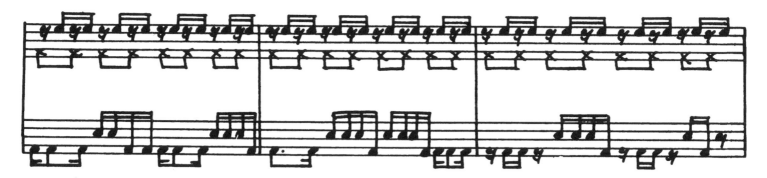

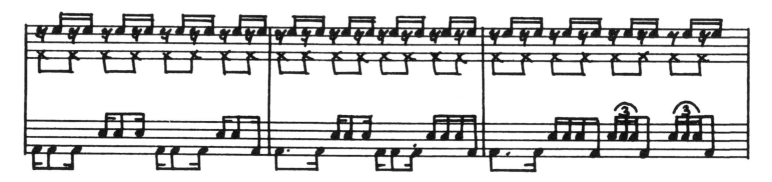

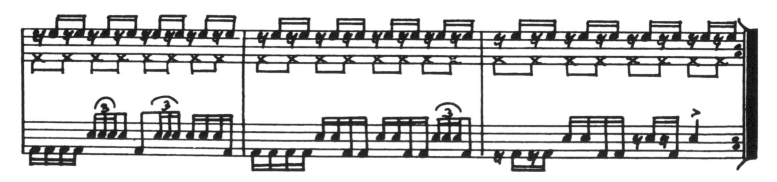

Funky 4/4 Feel

MED. FUNKY

SMALL AND LARGE
TOMS

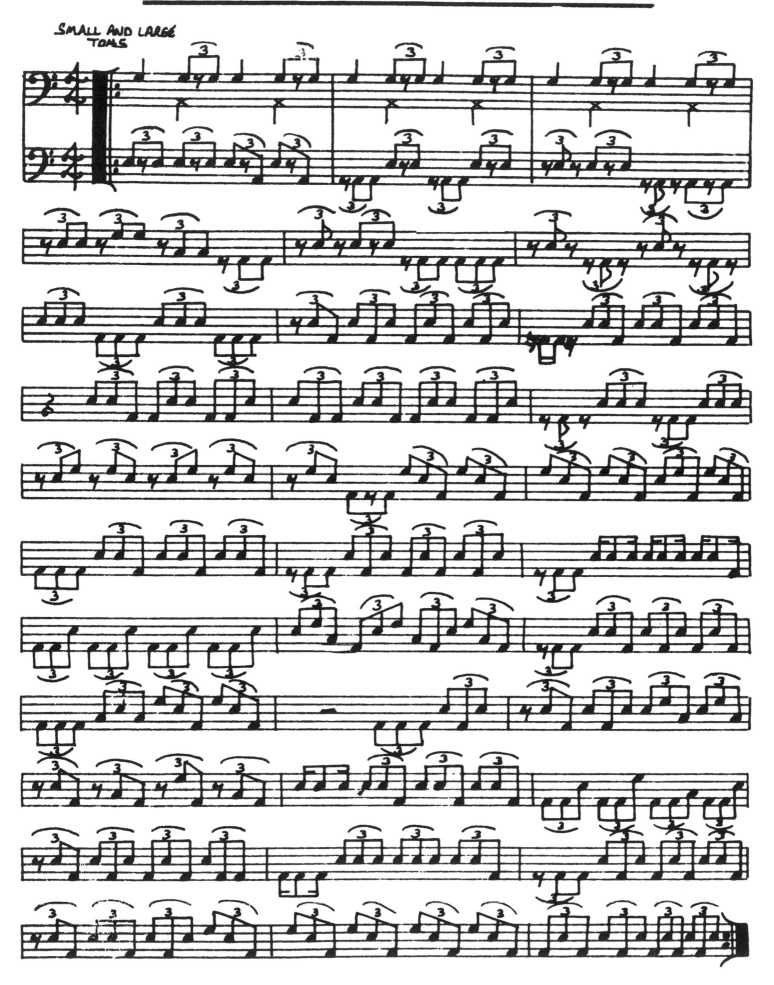

FUNKY BASS DRUM VAMPS - WITH COWBELL

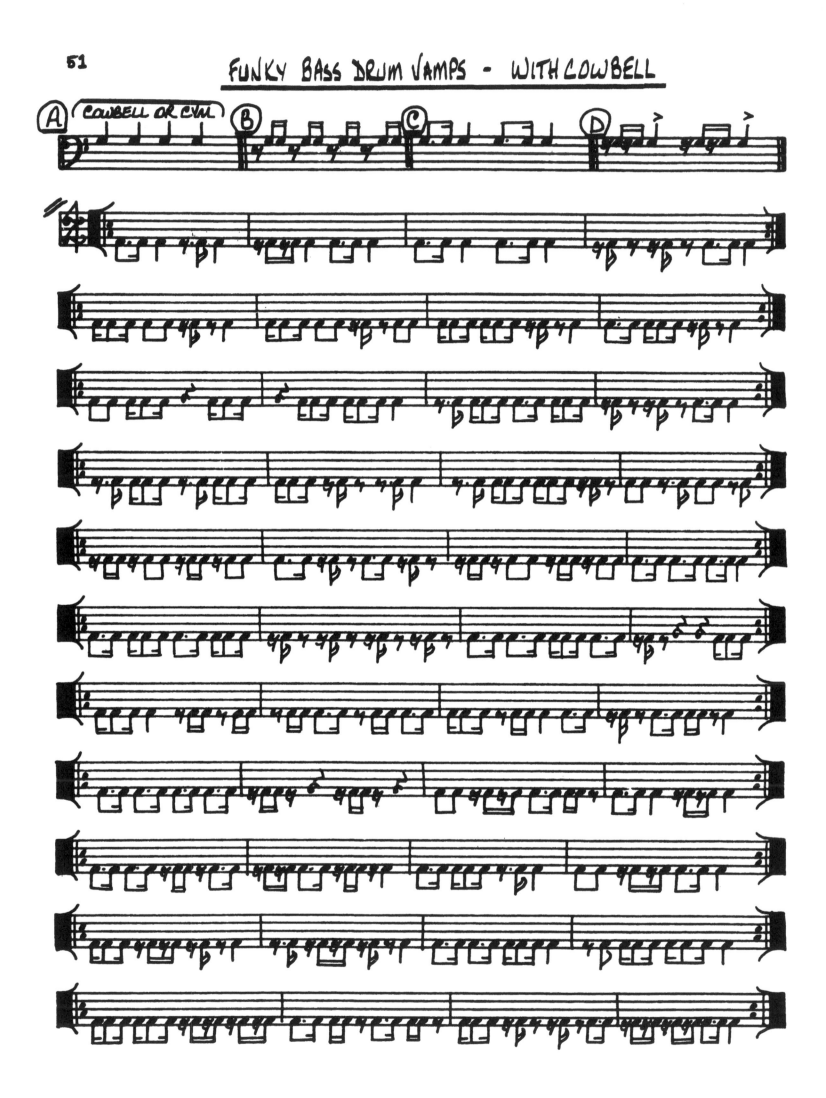

FOUR-BAR PHRASES
WITH JAZZ RIDE CYMBAL INDEPENDENCE

MED. GROOVE

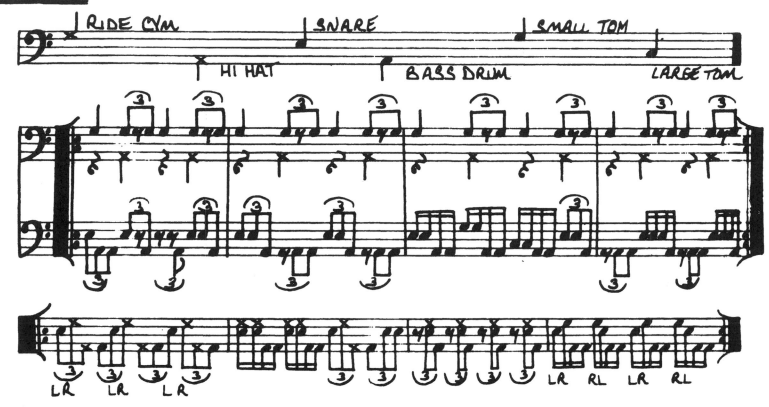

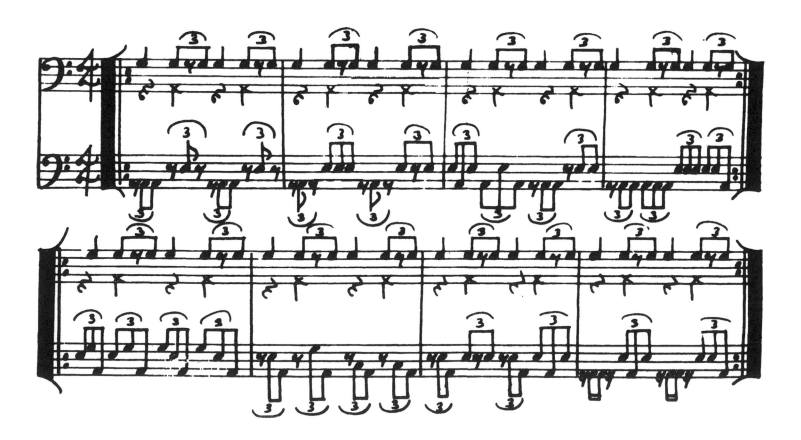

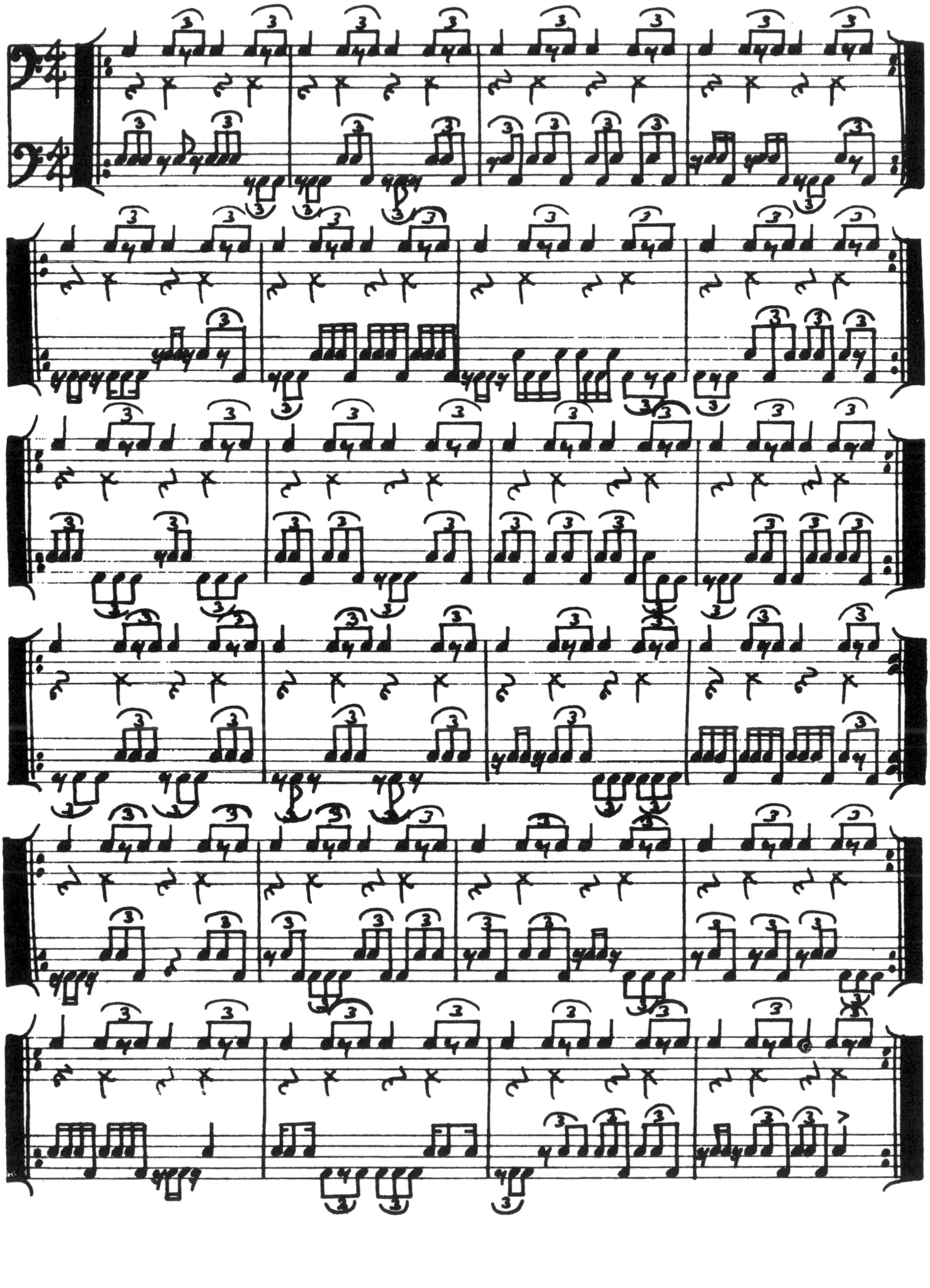

⁴₄ - ⁵₄ · Funk Lines with Three Ride Patterns

Play This Page Using All Three Ride Patterns

32·Bar Samba Excercise